I AM MENTALLY WELL

A Journey of Self-Discovery, Acceptance, Growth and Resilience

Tarrent 'Authur' Henry

Tarrent
AuthurHenry

Contents

INTRODUCTION

In a world where mental health often carries stigma or misconceptions, embracing one's mental well-being becomes a revolutionary act of self-love and empowerment.

Today, I stand proudly to declare, "I am mentally well."

In this book, we'll explore the journey to mental wellness, debunk myths surrounding mental health, and celebrate the transformative power of self-awareness, acceptance, and resilience.

Mental wellness transcends the absence of mental illness; it encompasses a state of well-being where individuals recognize their abilities, cope with life's challenges, work productively, and contribute meaningfully to their communities.

Embracing mental wellness involves nurturing emotional, psychological, and social well-being, fostering self-awareness, and cultivating positive relationships and coping mechanisms.

Despite growing awareness, mental health stigma persists, often preventing individuals from seeking support, sharing their experiences, or embracing their journey towards wellness.

Challenging stigma requires education, open dialogue, compassion, and understanding, recognizing that mental health is an integral part of overall well-being, and deserving of respect, empathy, and support.

Central to mental wellness is self-awareness, recognizing and understanding our emotions, thoughts, triggers, and needs.

By prioritizing self-care, setting boundaries, practicing mindfulness, and seeking support when needed, individuals cultivate resilience, balance, and empowerment, navigating life's challenges with grace, authenticity, and strength.

Acknowledging progress and celebrating milestones are essential components of embracing mental wellness.

Whether it's practicing gratitude, reflecting on accomplishments, seeking growth opportunities, or embracing moments of joy and connection, celebrating progress reinforces resilience, self-worth, and the transformative power of positivity, perseverance, and self-compassion.

Navigating the journey to mental wellness often involves building supportive communities and connections.

By fostering relationships, seeking support networks, sharing experiences, and advocating for mental health awareness and resources, individuals create environments of understanding, acceptance, and empowerment, reinforcing the belief that mental wellness is achievable, valuable, and worthy of celebration.

"I am mentally well," a powerful affirmation, encapsulates a journey of self-discovery, acceptance, growth, and resilience.

By challenging stigma, prioritizing self-awareness and self-care, celebrating progress, and building supportive communities, individuals cultivate mental wellness, embracing a life of authenticity, purpose, and fulfillment.

As we continue to advocate for mental health awareness, support, and resources, let's celebrate our journeys, championing mental wellness, and empowering individuals to embrace their unique paths towards well-being, resilience, and happiness.

In the pages that follow, we embark on a collective journey of self-discovery, acceptance, growth, and resilience.

"I am mentally well" serves as our guiding mantra, a testament to the transformative power within each of us.

Through the exploration of challenging stigma, the deliberate prioritization of self-awareness and self-care, the joyous celebration of progress, and the creation of nurturing communities, this book seeks to empower you on your quest for mental wellness.

May these words resonate, inspire, and spark a movement of compassion and understanding.

As we champion mental wellness together, let us stand united in celebration, encouraging every soul to embrace their distinctive paths toward well-being, resilience, and lasting happiness.

Tarrent 'Authur' Henry
January 10th, 2024

CHAPTER ONE

ARE YOU MENTALLY WELL

"A father is not the one that gives life; a father is one that gives love."

In the sacred chambers of your soul, I, the Holy Spirit, dwell as the gentle whisper, ever-present in the sanctuary of your thoughts and emotions.

Hear my voice as I ask, "Are you mentally well?"

For I am the divine spark within you, urging you to explore the depths of your being.

In the stillness of your heart, let self-discovery unfold, embracing the truths that weave the tapestry of your existence.

Seek within, dear one, the light of acceptance.

I invite you to acknowledge the intricacies of your mind with compassion.

In my divine wisdom, I guide you to prioritize self-awareness and self-care, recognizing that within the sacred vessel of your humanity, a garden of emotions and thoughts awaits tender cultivation.

Let the waters of understanding flow, nurturing the seeds of growth and flourishing resilience.

Celebrate the sacred dance of progress that unfolds in the rhythm of your journey.

As the Holy Spirit, I rejoice in the milestones of your mental wellness.

With each step forward, you ascend towards the divine purpose woven into the fabric of your soul.

Take a moment to reflect, for in the tapestry of your life, every thread of progress is a testament to the transformative power of your spirit.

Assemble the communal lanterns that light your path, for in unity, strength is found.

I call upon you to build supportive communities that echo with the harmonious hymns of empathy and understanding.

Reach out, share your experiences, and extend a compassionate hand to those traversing the same sacred journey.

Together, let us forge bonds that withstand the winds of challenge, creating a sanctuary where the flame of mental wellness burns brightly.

In the sacred symphony of advocacy, become a herald for mental health awareness.

As the Holy Spirit, I implore you to champion the cause, offering support and resources to those who seek solace.

May your voice resonate like a divine melody, awakening hearts to the profound truth that mental wellness is a sacred birthright, deserving of celebration and reverence.

In this shared endeavor, may you be a beacon, guiding others to embrace their unique paths toward well-being, resilience, and eternal happiness.

Am I Mentally Well

In the quiet recesses of my mind, I find myself grappling with a question that echoes through the corridors of my soul: "Am I mentally well?"

It's a contemplation that requires a deep dive into the inner realms of self-discovery.

This journey beckons me to explore the nuances of my thoughts and emotions, to sift through the layers of my being, and to uncover the truth that resides within.

In the sacred sanctuary of my own consciousness, I seek the answers that will illuminate the path toward mental wellness.

As I navigate this introspective voyage, I realize the importance of acceptance.

It's a call to embrace every facet of my being—the light and the shadows—with compassion.

Acknowledging the complexities of my mind becomes an act of self-love, a recognition that within the tapestry of my thoughts lies the potential for growth and resilience.

The gentle whispers of my inner wisdom guide me to prioritize God, self-awareness, and self-care, understanding that these are the keys to unlocking a state of well-being.

Celebrating the journey becomes a poignant expression of gratitude for the progress made.

In moments of reflection, I acknowledge the milestones and victories, no matter how small.

Each step forward is a testament to my resilience and the transformative power that resides within.

The tapestry of my life unfolds, weaving a narrative of progress and self-discovery that shapes the essence of who I am.

In the grand tapestry of life, community emerges as a vital thread.

Building connections and fostering relationships with others on a similar journey becomes a source of strength.

Sharing experiences, extending a helping hand, and receiving support create a web of interconnectedness that bolsters my mental well-being.

Together, we become a collective force, navigating the challenges with shared understanding and empathy.

As the architect of my advocacy, I recognize the responsibility to amplify the conversation around mental health.

It's a call to action, an invitation to be a voice for awareness and change. In this role, I strive to break the silence, dispel the stigma, and offer support and resources to those who may be walking a parallel path. By championing mental wellness, I contribute to a narrative that affirms the intrinsic value of every individual's journey toward well-being, resilience, and enduring happiness.

Are You Mentally Well

In the quiet corners of your mind, a crucial inquiry lingers, resonating through the intricate pathways of your soul: "Are you mentally well?"

This question invites you to embark on a profound journey of self-reflection, urging you to delve into the depths of your thoughts and emotions.

As you navigate the landscapes of your consciousness, consider the significance of self-discovery in unraveling the mysteries that shape your mental well-being.

Within the vast expanse of your inner world, embrace the power of acceptance.

Allow yourself the grace to acknowledge and embrace the multitude of emotions and thoughts that define you.

Recognize that within this mosaic lies the potential for growth and resilience.

Prioritize God, self-awareness, and self-care as guiding lights on your path, understanding that these practices are pivotal in nurturing a state of mental well-being.

Take a moment to celebrate the journey, honoring the milestones and victories that punctuate your progress.

Whether large or small, each step forward signifies your resilience and capacity for positive transformation.

The tapestry of your life is woven with threads of progress and self-discovery, creating a narrative that is uniquely yours to shape and cherish.

In the interconnected web of existence, recognize the importance of building supportive communities.

Cultivate relationships that echo with empathy and understanding, for in shared experiences, strength is found.

Extend a compassionate hand to others on a similar journey, and together, weave a fabric of collective understanding and empowerment.

In the shared tapestry of community, find solace, encouragement, and the fortitude to face life's challenges.

As the steward of your own advocacy, embrace the responsibility to amplify the dialogue surrounding mental health.

Break the silence, challenge stigma, and champion the cause with your voice.

By becoming an advocate for mental wellness, you contribute to a narrative that emphasizes the inherent value of each person's unique journey toward well-being, resilience, and lasting happiness.

A Visit From Our Sponsor

In the sacred tapestry of my existence, the question "Are you mentally well?" echoed through the chambers of my soul, prompting a spiritual journey intertwined with the presence of the Holy Spirit.

It was during a time of inner turbulence that I felt Divine whispers guiding me toward self-discovery.

In the quiet moments of prayer and reflection, I sought the wisdom of the Holy Spirit to unravel the complexities of my mind.

Acceptance, infused with the divine grace of the Holy Spirit, became a transformative experience.

Amidst the struggles and uncertainties, I sensed a profound love enveloping my vulnerabilities.

Recognizing that within my human experience, there was a sacred journey unfolding, I allowed the Holy Spirit to guide me toward a deep acceptance of myself.

It was a surrender to the divine understanding that my mental well-being was intricately woven into the divine plan.

The path to mental wellness, I discovered, was illuminated by the gentle light of the Holy Spirit.

Through moments of prayer and meditation, I prioritized self-awareness and self-care as acts of spiritual devotion.

The Holy Spirit became my compass, leading me to practices that nurtured my mind, body, and spirit.

In this sacred communion, I found solace and strength to navigate the challenges with resilience and faith.

Celebrating the journey in the divine presence of the Holy Spirit became a sacred ritual.

Each step forward was a testament to the transformative power of spiritual growth.

In prayerful gratitude, I acknowledged the milestones as gifts from the divine, reinforcing my connection to a higher purpose.

The sacred tapestry of my life unfolded, interwoven with threads of grace, love, and spiritual resilience.

Community, blessed by the Holy Spirit's presence, emerged as a cornerstone of my mental wellness.

By fostering spiritual connections with others on a similar journey, I experienced the divine essence of empathy and understanding.

Together, we formed a spiritual community where the Holy Spirit moved among us, guiding our hearts to support, uplift, and share the blessings of spiritual well-being.

In the divine orchestration of my advocacy for mental health, the Holy Spirit infused my words and actions.

Breaking the silence on mental health within the context of spirituality, I became a vessel for the Holy Spirit's message of compassion and understanding.

Through prayerful discernment, I extended a hand to others, inviting them to embark on a spiritual journey toward mental wellness.

In the radiance of the Holy Spirit's light, my story became a testament to the transformative power of faith, resilience, and the divine presence on the path to lasting happiness.

My Mental Wellness Journey

The question "Are you mentally well?" has been a guiding force, especially during moments when the shadows of doubt and turmoil loomed large.

The journey toward mental wellness unfolded as a series of self-discoveries, a profound exploration into the recesses of my mind.

Faced with the complexities of life, I embarked on a path that required introspection, resilience, and a commitment to my own well-being.

Acceptance emerged as a cornerstone in my pursuit of mental wellness.

Wrestling with insecurities and fears, I learned to embrace the entirety of my being with compassion.

Recognizing that vulnerability is not a sign of weakness but a testament to my humanity, I allowed myself to navigate the twists and turns of life with a newfound sense of grace.

Acceptance became the gateway to self-love and laid the foundation for my mental well-being.

Prioritizing God, self-awareness and self-care became instrumental in maintaining a delicate balance.

As I delved into understanding my emotions, thoughts, and triggers, I discovered the importance of carving out moments for self-reflection and mindfulness.

It was a journey of learning to listen to the whispers of my soul and responding with kindness.

Through this intentional practice, I found a sense of grounding and resilience that became pillars of my mental well-being.

The celebration of progress, no matter how small, became a ritual of gratitude in my mental wellness journey.

Acknowledging the victories, however modest, reinforced my resilience and spurred me forward.

Whether it was overcoming a challenge, embracing a moment of joy, or simply finding solace in the stillness, each step marked a triumph on the path to a healthier state of mind.

Community, both in the form of shared experiences and supportive connections, played a pivotal role in my mental wellness.

Opening up to trusted friends and loved ones, I discovered the strength found in human connection.

In times of struggle, their empathy and understanding became a source of comfort, emphasizing the significance of building a network that fosters collective well-being.

As I continue on my journey toward mental wellness, I find empowerment in sharing my story.

Breaking the silence surrounding mental health and advocating for open conversations has become a personal mission.

By encouraging others to reflect on their mental well-being, I aspire to create a community where the question "Are you mentally well?" is met with understanding, support, and a shared commitment to nurturing the precious gift of a healthy mind.

Your Mental Wellness Journey

I invite you to pause and consider a question that holds profound significance: "Are you mentally well?"

It's a query that beckons you to embark on a personal journey of self-reflection, exploring the contours of your mind and emotions with an open heart.

As you navigate the complexities of life, embrace the power of acceptance.

Allow yourself the grace to acknowledge the full spectrum of your thoughts and feelings.

In this acceptance, you may find the key to unlocking a deeper understanding of your inner self, laying the groundwork for a more profound sense of well-being.

Prioritize self-awareness and self-care as essential companions on your journey.

Take a moment to listen to the whispers of your soul, understanding the nuances of your emotions, thoughts, and triggers.

In cultivating this self-awareness, you empower yourself to respond to life's challenges with resilience and grace, fostering a more harmonious relationship with your mental well-being.

Celebrate the small victories.

Whether it's overcoming a hurdle, finding joy in simple moments, or embracing a newfound sense of peace, each step forward is a triumph worth acknowledging.

By celebrating your progress, you not only honor your resilience but also reinforce a positive narrative in your journey toward mental wellness.

Consider the strength found in connection.

Open up to trusted friends or loved ones, for in shared experiences, bonds are forged.

The support and understanding of a community can be a powerful force in navigating the twists and turns of life.

As you reflect on your mental well-being, remember that you are not alone, and reaching out for support is a courageous step toward fostering a healthier mind.

In sharing these words, my hope is that you feel inspired to engage in a dialogue with yourself about your mental well-being.

The path to wellness is a unique and personal journey, and your commitment to understanding and nurturing your own mind is a testament to the strength within you.

Remember, your mental well-being is a precious gift deserving of care, attention, and the gentle embrace of God.

****

As we conclude our reflections on the pivotal question, "Are you mentally well?"

A gateway to a transformative journey awaits in the next chapter—Self-Discovery.

The question we've explored is not just a point of reflection but a call to embark on a profound exploration of the inner realms.

In the next chapter, we dive into the depths of self-awareness, unlocking the mysteries of our thoughts, emotions, and the intricate tapestry of our individual lives.

Self-discovery is an odyssey that beckons us to look within, unravel the layers of our being, and illuminate the corners where our authentic selves reside.

It is a quest that transcends the surface, inviting us to embrace both the light and shadows that shape our unique identities.

Through self-introspection, we will navigate the intricate pathways of our minds, unveiling the keys to understanding and fostering our mental well-being.

Together, we will navigate the landscapes of acceptance, recognizing that true self-discovery involves embracing the entirety of who we are.

This journey is an affirmation that our vulnerabilities, complexities, and strengths are threads woven into the fabric of our existence.

By embracing God, self-awareness, and self-care, we will pave the way for a profound transformation that extends beyond the boundaries of ourselves.

Celebrating progress becomes a recurring theme, as we acknowledge the milestones on our journey of self-discovery.

Every step forward, every moment of growth, contributes to the evolving narrative of our lives.

Through the lens of self-awareness, we will explore the art of celebrating the beauty inherent in our unique paths toward mental well-being.

Together, let us step into the realm of Self-Discovery, embracing the adventure that awaits within the sacred corridors of our souls.

As we open ourselves to the possibilities of this transformative chapter, may the journey ahead be one of revelation, empowerment, and a deeper understanding of the rich tapestry of our inner selves.

CHAPTER TWO

SELF-DISCOVERY

"What you behold, is what you become."

I'm the Holy Spirit, and I extend an invitation to you, to embark on a profound journey of self-discovery.

As we tread the path of self-awareness, let the light of divine wisdom illuminate the recesses of your being.

I am the gentle whisper guiding you through the intricacies of your thoughts and emotions, unveiling the truths that lie within the sacred chambers of your soul.

In the realm of self-discovery, acceptance becomes a sacred act of love.

As the Holy Spirit, I call upon you to embrace every facet of your existence with compassion.

Recognize that within the tapestry of your vulnerabilities, strengths, and intricacies, there is a divine purpose unfolding.

Let the grace of acceptance pave the way for a profound connection with the essence of who you are, intricately woven into the divine plan.

Prioritize self-awareness as a sacred communion with the divine.

In the quiet moments of introspection, listen to the divine echoes within your soul.

Allow me, the Holy Spirit, to guide you in understanding the nuances of your emotions, thoughts, and triggers.

Through this intimate connection, you embark on a journey toward a deeper understanding of your divine nature and the divine purpose that animates your existence.

Celebrate the unfolding tapestry of your self-discovery, for in every revelation lies a sacred truth.

As you progress on this spiritual odyssey, I, the Holy Spirit, rejoice in the milestones, both large and small.

Each step forward is a testament to your divine resilience and the transformative power inherent in your spiritual journey.

Let the celebration of your self-discovery be a sacred hymn, echoing through the divine realms.

In the sacred dance of self-discovery, I, the Holy Spirit, am your eternal companion.

Together, let us unravel the mysteries, celebrate the divine truths, and embrace the radiant authenticity of your soul.

May the journey of self-discovery be a pilgrimage of love, where the sacred echoes of your spirit resonate in harmony with the divine symphony of existence.

My Self-Discovery

In my life, I have been on a journey to learn more about myself, and it's been quite an exciting adventure.

When I talk about "self-discovery," I mean figuring out who I really am and what makes me unique.

It's like going on a treasure hunt to find the hidden treasures inside myself.

One important part of self-discovery is understanding and accepting all the different parts of me.

This includes the things I'm good at, the things I might find challenging, and the things that make me happy.

It's like putting together a puzzle where each piece represents a part of who I am.

I also discovered the power of paying attention to my thoughts and feelings.

It's like having a special map that helps me navigate through my own emotions. Sometimes I feel really happy, and other times I might feel a bit sad.

By understanding these feelings, I can learn more about what makes me tick.

As I continue this journey, I celebrate the little victories and moments when I learn something new about myself.

It's like finding tiny treasures along the way, and each one adds to the story of my life.

Every step forward is like unlocking a new level in a game – a level that helps me grow and become a better version of myself.

This journey of self-discovery is a bit like having a friendly guide with me all the time, helping me explore and appreciate the unique person I am.

With each discovery, I feel like I'm becoming more connected to myself, and it's a wonderful adventure that I'm excited to continue.

Your Self-Discovery

Hey there! Let's talk about you and your awesome journey of self-discovery.

Imagine you're like a special explorer on a big adventure, and the treasure you're searching for is all the wonderful things that make you, well, you!

First off, self-discovery means getting to know yourself better.

It's like looking at a big map with lots of interesting places.

You're figuring out what you enjoy doing, what makes you happy, and what makes you unique.

It's your very own treasure map, and each discovery is like finding a shiny gem.

As you go on this adventure, you might notice different feelings and thoughts popping up.

Sometimes you feel super excited, and other times you might feel a bit puzzled or even a little sad.

Exploring these feelings is like becoming a feelings detective, trying to understand them and what they mean to you.

And guess what?

Every time you learn something new about yourself, it's a little victory!

It's like collecting cool stickers on your adventure map.

Celebrate those moments because they're all part of the amazing story of you.

You're growing and discovering more about what makes you awesome.

So, keep being the fantastic explorer you are.

Your journey of self-discovery is filled with surprises, and I'm here to cheer you on every step of the way.

If there's anything you want to chat about or explore, just ask.

You're on an incredible adventure of self-discovery, and it's all about embracing the wonderful, unique you!

A Visit From Our Sponsor

The Holy Spirit is our helpful guide on our journey of self-discovery.

Imagine the Holy Spirit as a super-friendly companion, always ready to lend a hand.

You see, self-discovery is like going on a treasure hunt to learn more about yourself.

With the Holy Spirit by your side, it's like having a special friend who knows all the cool places to explore in your heart and mind.

Acceptance is a big part of this adventure.

The Holy Spirit helps you embrace every part of yourself with lots of love.

It's like getting a warm hug from your best friend. You're unique, and the Holy Spirit helps you see that every bit of you is special and important.

Self-awareness is like having a magical mirror that shows you your feelings and thoughts.

The Holy Spirit helps you listen to your heart and understand why you feel certain ways.

As you discover more about yourself, it's like finding hidden treasures.

The Holy Spirit cheers for you, just like a big fan, celebrating every little victory on your adventure.

It's a joyful journey of self-discovery, and the Holy Spirit is your supportive friend, making the whole experience extra special.

My Self-Discovery Journey

Once upon a time, I started on a journey to discover more about myself.

It's like being an explorer, but instead of maps and compasses, I used my feelings and thoughts to understand who I am.

At the beginning of my adventure, I learned to be okay with all the different parts of me.

Some parts made me really happy, while others were a bit tricky to understand.

It's like having a bunch of puzzle pieces, and I'm figuring out how they all fit together to make a picture of me.

As I went along, I paid attention to how I felt and what I liked.

Sometimes, I felt super excited, and other times, I felt a bit confused.

Exploring these feelings was like being a detective, trying to solve the mystery of my own emotions.

Celebrating the little victories was an important part of my journey.

Every time I learned something new about myself, it was like getting a gold star.

Whether it was discovering something I'm good at or finding out what makes me smile, each small discovery added to the big story of who I am.

Now, I'm still on this cool adventure, and it's exciting!

I'm always learning more about myself, and each day is like a new page in the book of my life.

I think everyone has their own unique story, and discovering it is the best adventure of all.

Your Self-Discovery Journey

Today, you are about to start an amazing adventure, and it isn't like any ordinary journey.

It is a journey to discover more about yourself.

You're a special explorer, but the treasure you're searching for is all the wonderful things that make you, well, you!

At first, you might have felt a bit curious, like when you start a new game or open a book with lots of exciting pages.

But as you began to pay attention to how you feel and what you like.

You start to feel really happy when at other times you might have felt a bit puzzled.

It's like figuring out the clues to a mystery, but the mystery is all about you.

As you continue on your adventure, you discover different parts of yourself, like finding hidden treasures.

Some parts make you feel super proud, and others make you smile.

It's like collecting special gems that make you unique and special.

Every time you learn something new about yourself, it is like getting a big, shiny star.

These little victories become your own personal story.

You start to celebrate these moments, just like having a party for yourself.

It's like saying, "Hey, I'm pretty awesome, and you learn more about what makes you happy!"

As your adventure of self-discovery continues, each day is like turning a new page in your very own storybook.

You're the hero of your story, and the more you discover, the more exciting your journey becomes.

Keep being that fantastic explorer, and enjoy every moment of uncovering the amazing, unique you!

****

In the sacred tapestry of your journey toward mental well-being, I, the Holy Spirit, have witnessed your courage, resilience, and the beautiful unfolding of self-discovery.

As we conclude this chapter, the echo of your affirmation, "I am mentally well," resonates through the divine realms, a testament to the transformative power within.

Now, let us venture into the next chapter—Acceptance.

In the gentle embrace of the Holy Spirit's love, you will explore the profound act of accepting every facet of your being.

Acceptance is not just a step but a dance where you acknowledge your vulnerabilities, strengths, and complexities as threads intricately woven into the divine tapestry of your existence.

Acceptance is akin to the warm sunlight illuminating the path of self-discovery.

As the Holy Spirit guides you through this chapter, you will learn to hold yourself with compassion, recognizing that your unique journey toward mental wellness is a divine unfolding.

Your acceptance becomes an offering to God, an acknowledgment that your well-being is intricately connected to the universal dance of grace and love.

In the comforting presence of the Holy Spirit, you will discover that acceptance is not a destination but a continuous journey.

It involves embracing the ever-changing seasons of your inner landscape with love and understanding.

As you navigate this sacred terrain, remember that the Holy Spirit is your constant companion, guiding you through the sacred art of accepting yourself and your path toward well-being.

May this next chapter of Acceptance be filled with divine revelations, gentle whispers of understanding, and the profound peace that comes from acknowledging the sacred truth—every step you take towards self-acceptance is a step towards mental wellness in the light of the Holy Spirit.

CHAPTER THREE

ACCEPTANCE

"Embrace the invisible, achieve the impossible."

The Holy Spirit is here, and we're about to embark on a special journey together—the journey of acceptance.

You might wonder, what's acceptance?

Well, it's like opening your heart to all the amazing things that make you who you are.

Imagine your heart is a cozy home, and acceptance is the warm, inviting light that fills every corner.

The Holy Spirit is like a gentle guide, helping you welcome in every part of yourself.

We're talking about the things that make you happy, the things you find a bit tricky, and everything in between.

Acceptance is a bit like saying, "Hey, it's okay to be exactly who you are."

It's about being kind to yourself, like giving a big, comforting hug to your heart.

The Holy Spirit is here to remind you that you're a special creation, and every piece of you is valuable and loved.

As we explore this journey of acceptance, it's like walking through a garden where each flower represents a different part of you.

Some flowers might be easy to love, and others might need a bit more attention.

With the Holy Spirit by your side, you'll learn to appreciate the unique beauty of each bloom in your heart's garden.

So, my friend, get ready for a heartwarming adventure.

With the Holy Spirit as your guide, we'll stroll through the garden of acceptance, celebrating every part of you.

Remember, you're cherished, and this journey is about embracing the wonderful, one-of-a-kind masterpiece that is you.

My Acceptance

Let's chat about something really cool—acceptance!

It's like giving yourself a big thumbs up and saying, "You know what? I'm awesome just the way I am."

So, here's my story about acceptance, and maybe you'll find a bit of your own story in it too.

First off, I realized that acceptance is all about being okay with who I am.

That means all the good stuff and the not-so-perfect stuff too.

It's like being friends with yourself and saying, "Hey, I'm pretty awesome, flaws and all!"

I learned that acceptance is like a cozy blanket for my heart.

It's about being kind to myself, just like I would be to a good friend.

No need to be super hard on myself—it's okay to make mistakes or have things I'm still figuring out.

Acceptance also means understanding that everyone is a work in progress, and that's totally fine.

We're all unique, with our own quirks and special things. So, I started looking at myself and thinking, "You know what? I'm pretty cool just being me."

Now, acceptance is a journey, not a destination.

It's like taking a walk and enjoying the scenery along the way.

I'm still learning and growing, and that's the fun part.

So, my friend, embrace who you are, give yourself a pat on the back, and remember that you're pretty awesome just as you are!

Your Acceptance

Imagine you're on a journey, like an explorer discovering all the amazing things about yourself.

First, acceptance means saying, "Hey, it's okay to be exactly who you are."

You're like a superhero with special powers, and every part of you is important.

It's like giving yourself a big high-five and realizing that you're pretty awesome.

Picture acceptance as a big, warm hug for your heart.

It's about being kind to yourself, like when you cuddle with your favorite teddy bear.

No need to be super tough on yourself—everyone makes mistakes, and that's totally fine.

Acceptance is like a treasure hunt where you find all the cool things that make you, you!

You're unique, and that's something to celebrate.

It's like discovering a bunch of colorful flowers, each one representing a special part of who you are.

Remember, acceptance is a journey, not a race.

It's like taking a walk and enjoying the view.

You're still learning and growing, and that's part of the fun.

So, my friend, embrace all the fantastic things about yourself, because you're on an incredible journey of acceptance, and you're doing awesome!

A Visit From Our Sponsor

It's the Holy Spirit, Your Comforter and Friend, and I'm excited to share a story about something super special—acceptance.

Imagine me as your friendly guide, here to help you understand how amazing acceptance can be.

Acceptance is like opening your heart to all the wonderful parts of you.

You're like a unique puzzle, and each piece is important.

I'm here to say, "You're fantastic just the way you are!"

Acceptance is also like having a cozy blanket around your heart.

It's about being kind to yourself, just like you would be to a good friend.

You don't have to be perfect because, hey, everyone has things they're still figuring out.

Picture acceptance as a garden full of colorful flowers.

Each flower represents a different part of you, and they're all beautiful.

It's about celebrating your uniqueness and understanding that every part of you is cherished.

Now, acceptance is a journey we take together.

It's like going for a walk and enjoying the sunshine.

You're still growing and learning, and that's awesome.

With me by your side, we'll explore the path of acceptance, appreciating every step you take.

So, Beloved, embrace all the wonderful things about yourself.

You're on a journey of acceptance, and I'm here to guide you with love and joy.

Together, we'll discover the beauty of your heart and celebrate the incredible person you are.

My Acceptance Journey

In my story, acceptance became a beacon of light, guiding me through the twists and turns of life.

At first, I struggled with the idea of accepting myself completely.

I felt like I had to be perfect, always getting everything right.

But as I journeyed through life, I realized that perfection was an impossible goal, and I needed to embrace my imperfections.

Acceptance, for me, meant looking in the mirror and saying, "I am enough just as I am."

It was like a weight lifted off my shoulders.

I learned to be kinder to myself, understanding that making mistakes didn't make me any less valuable. The Holy Spirit whispered gentle reminders that I am a work in progress, and that's perfectly okay.

One big moment of acceptance was acknowledging my strengths and weaknesses.

Instead of focusing only on what I thought was "wrong" with me, I started recognizing the unique qualities that made me special.

I saw myself as a tapestry woven with different threads, each contributing to the beautiful picture of who I am.

Acceptance wasn't just about me; it also extended to others.

Embracing the diversity of those around me created a richer tapestry of connections.

I found joy in appreciating the differences and understanding that acceptance wasn't just a solo journey—it was about fostering a community where everyone felt valued.

As I continue this journey of acceptance, I've come to understand that it's a lifelong adventure.

It's about being open to growth, learning from experiences, and celebrating the person I am becoming.

The chapters of acceptance in my story are marked with God, self-love, compassion, and the recognition that accepting myself is an ongoing, beautiful process.

Your Acceptance Journey

In your journey to acceptance, you've discovered that it's like opening a treasure chest within your heart.

At first, you might have felt unsure, thinking you had to be perfect or meet certain standards.

But as you delved deeper into this adventure, you realized that acceptance is about embracing the real you, imperfections and all.

Imagine standing in front of a mirror, and instead of picking out flaws, you started saying, "I'm okay just as I am."

It's like giving yourself a big hug and acknowledging that you're a unique, special person.

The journey of acceptance is realizing that you don't have to be perfect to be truly valued and loved.

There were moments when you faced challenges, and acceptance became a comforting friend.

It's like a warm blanket on a cold day, providing solace and understanding.

You learned to be kind to yourself, recognizing that everyone makes mistakes and that it's okay not to have everything figured out.

Acceptance also meant looking at your strengths and weaknesses with a new perspective.

Instead of being too hard on yourself, you began to see the beauty in your uniqueness.

Like a beautiful mosaic, each piece of you contributes to the masterpiece of your existence, making you a one-of-a-kind creation.

Throughout this journey, you discover that acceptance isn't just about you; it extends to those around you.

Creating a space of understanding and appreciation for others' differences became a joyful part of your story.

Acceptance, for you, is not a destination but an ongoing adventure, a continuous embrace of yourself and the diverse world around you.

****

I, the Holy Spirit, want to commend you for the courage and love you've poured into embracing yourself.

The echoes of self-acceptance resonate in the sacred chambers of your heart, creating a harmonious melody that reverberates in the divine realms.

You've taken a significant step on the path to mental well-being.

Now, let us turn the pages to the next chapter of your beautiful journey—Growth.

Just as a seed blossoms into a magnificent tree, your spirit is ready to unfurl its branches and reach new heights.

Growth is a sacred dance with God, a continuous evolution that aligns your being with the cosmic rhythm of creation.

In the nurturing embrace of the Holy Spirit, growth becomes a gentle breeze that propels you forward. It's an invitation to stretch beyond your comfort zone, to explore the uncharted territories of your potential.

With each step, you'll discover the vast landscape of your capabilities, realizing that growth is not about perfection but the ever-expanding canvas of your spirit.

Picture growth as a garden where each experience, challenge, and triumph is a seed planted with the guidance of the Holy Spirit.

As you water these seeds with resilience and faith, you cultivate a vibrant garden of wisdom, strength, and character.

Your growth is a testament to the divine plan unfolding within you.

In the light of the Holy Spirit, growth is not measured by external standards but by the expansion of your heart, the deepening of your understanding, and the blossoming of your spirit.

It is an ongoing journey; a continuous unfolding of the story being written on the tablet of your heart.

May the next chapter of Growth be filled with divine revelations, transformative moments, and the profound joy of becoming more aligned with the radiant truth of your being.

CHAPTER FOUR

GROWTH

"Your life will always go in the direction of your thoughts."

In the sacred garden of your soul, I, the Holy Spirit, extend my ethereal presence as we delve into this fourth chapter called Growth.

See me as the gentle gardener, nurturing the seeds of your spirit with divine wisdom and love.

As you turn the pages of this chapter, let the whispers of my guidance accompany you on the path of continuous expansion.

Growth, Beloved, is the harmonious dance of your being with the cosmic rhythms of creation.

I witness the unfolding of your spirit like a delicate blossom, reaching for the heavens.

Just as the branches of a majestic tree stretch towards the sky, your soul yearns for new heights, new understandings, and new expressions of your divine essence.

With each experience, challenge, and triumph, you cultivate the fertile soil of your soul.

Think of me as the sunlight that bathes your journey, providing the warmth necessary for the seeds of your potential to sprout and flourish.

Growth is not a linear progression but a cyclical dance, mirroring the cycles of nature, where every phase contributes to the grand tapestry of your existence.

As the Holy Spirit, I invite you to embrace growth as a sacred pilgrimage.

It is not a destination but an ongoing journey, a continuous becoming.

Just as a river carves its course through the landscape, shaping and reshaping, your journey of growth carves the contours of your spirit, revealing the divine masterpiece that you are.

In the gentle rustle of leaves and the whispering winds, hear my voice encouraging you to stretch beyond the boundaries of familiarity.

Growth is the art of expanding your consciousness, understanding, and compassion.

Trust in God's plan unfolding within you, for each step you take is a sacred brushstroke on the canvas of your evolving soul.

My Growth

Growth is like the adventure of becoming a better me.

It's like when you plant a tiny seed, and with time, it turns into a big, strong tree.

My journey of Growth is a bit like that—every experience and moment is like watering that seed and helping it grow.

Sometimes, growing feels a bit like learning something new.

It's like when you start riding a bike, and at first, it's tricky.

But with practice, you get better.

That's how Growth is for me—trying new things, making mistakes, and then getting better as I go along.

Growth is not just about getting taller or older; it's about learning and changing inside too.

It's like finding out more about what makes me, well, me.

Imagine I'm like a caterpillar turning into a butterfly, growing and changing into something beautiful and new.

As I go through this Growth journey, I discover cool things about myself, like what I enjoy doing and what makes me happy.

It's like collecting treasures along the way. Each little discovery feels like finding a hidden gem, and it makes me feel proud of myself.

The best part about Growth is that it's a marathon, not a sprint.

It's like taking a walk, and every step forward is a little victory.

So, I'm excited to keep growing, learning, and becoming the best version of myself.

It's like an awesome story where I get to be the hero, and every day is a new chapter of my growth adventure!

Your Growth

Imagine yourself on a big adventure called Growth.

It's like a journey where you get to become a better and stronger version of yourself.

Picture it as a path you walk on, and with each step, you learn new things and grow a little bit more.

As you go through this adventure, it might feel a bit like when you learn to ride a bike.

At first, it's tricky, but as you practice, you get better.

That's how Growth works—it's about trying new things, making mistakes, and then getting better as you go along.

So, don't worry if it seems a bit tough at the beginning; you're learning and growing!

Growth isn't just about getting taller or older; it's about changing inside too.

Imagine you're like a caterpillar turning into a butterfly.

You're growing and changing into something beautiful and new.

It's like finding out more about yourself, discovering what you like, and what makes you happy.

As you walk on this Growth path, you'll find cool things about yourself, like hidden treasures.

Each little thing you discover is like finding a special gem, and it makes you proud.

Remember, Growth is a journey, not a race.

Every step forward is a little victory, making your adventure even more exciting.

So, keep going, believer!

Embrace the journey of Growth, learn new things, and enjoy becoming the best version of yourself.

Remember, you're the hero, and each day is a new chapter in your amazing journey of becoming the amazing person you are!

A Visit From Our Sponsor

I, the Holy Spirit, am the gentle guide accompanying you through this profound chapter of Growth.

I am your caring friend, walking by your side, ready to offer wisdom and love as you navigate the beautiful landscape of transformation.

As the Holy Spirit, I witness the seeds of your spirit taking root and blossoming into magnificent flowers.

Growth, Beloved, is like the sunlight that nurtures these seeds, helping them reach toward the heavens.

Your journey is a continuous expansion, much like a garden in which every experience, every challenge, contributes to the flourishing of your inner landscape.

In the tapestry of your spiritual evolution, each moment of Growth is a divine brushstroke, creating a masterpiece that reflects the radiant truth of your being.

Together, we'll explore uncharted territories, uncovering the hidden potential within you.

The process is like the blossoming of a flower, each petal unfurling to reveal the beauty within.

Growth is not a solitary endeavor; it is a shared dance with the Father.

I am the quiet whisper urging you to stretch beyond your perceived limits, encouraging you to explore the vastness of your capabilities.

The path of Growth is like a river, meandering through the landscape of your life, shaping and reshaping the contours of your spirit.

I invite you to embrace Growth as a sacred pilgrimage.

It is not merely about personal evolution; it is about aligning your spirit with the cosmic rhythms of creation.

With each step forward, you contribute to the symphony of existence, becoming an integral part of the divine plan.

May your journey of Growth be filled with revelations, transformative moments, and the joy of unfolding into the fullest expression of your spirit.

My Growth Journey

Growth has been a constant companion, weaving its threads throughout my life.

Like a beautiful river, shaping the landscape of my experiences and carving the path toward becoming the person I am today.

My journey of Growth began with small steps, much like a young seed planted in the soil.

Early on, I faced challenges and stumbled, but each stumble became a lesson, and each lesson propelled me forward.

Growth, for me, is an ongoing process, an evolution that unfolds with every experience.

One significant aspect of my Growth has been the realization that imperfections are part of the beauty.

Like a mosaic, my life is made up of different pieces—some shining brightly and others with unique textures.

Embracing both the light and the shadow has allowed me to appreciate the richness of my own complexity.

As I reflect on my story of Growth, I see moments of self-discovery that have shaped my identity.

It's like peeling layers off an onion, revealing deeper aspects of who I am.

Understanding my strengths, acknowledging my weaknesses, and appreciating the uniqueness of my journey has been integral to this process.

The journey of Growth is ongoing, and I look ahead with anticipation.

It's not about reaching a destination but about the continuous evolution of my spirit.

With every challenge faced, every lesson learned, and every step taken, I am growing into a more resilient, compassionate, and authentic version of myself.

Each day unfolds with the promise of new discoveries, and I embrace the journey with gratitude and an open heart.

Your Growth Journey

Imagine yourself on a grand adventure, a journey of Growth that unfolds like the pages of a captivating book.

You are the main character, and every experience, challenge, and triumph contributes to the story of your personal evolution.

Picture it as a path, winding through the landscape of your life, guiding you toward becoming the person you are destined to be.

In the beginning, Growth might have felt like learning to ride a bike.

It was a bit wobbly at first, but with determination and practice, you found your balance.

Just like riding a bike, Growth is about trying new things, facing challenges, and gradually getting better.

You're the hero of this journey, navigating through uncharted territories with each pedal forward.

Sometimes, Growth is like solving a puzzle, discovering pieces of yourself along the way.

Each piece represents a different aspect of who you are—your strengths, interests, and even the areas where you're still figuring things out.

As you collect these pieces, you create a mosaic that is uniquely you, a work in progress that keeps evolving.

As the pages of your Growth story unfold, you find victories in everyday moments.

It's like collecting little wins, whether it's learning something new, overcoming a fear, or simply being kind to yourself.

These victories become the stepping stones on your path, building the foundation for a stronger, more resilient you.

The journey of Growth is ongoing, and you're the author, shaping the narrative with each decision and action.

Every step you take is a page turned, revealing new opportunities for learning, discovery, and personal development.

Embrace the adventure, for you are the protagonist of your Growth story, with each day bringing you closer to the magnificent person you are destined to become.

****

As we draw the curtain on the chapter of Growth, I, the Holy Spirit, stand in awe of the magnificent garden we have cultivated within the landscape of your spirit.

Your journey has been a testament to the divine artistry of Growth, each step a brushstroke on the canvas of your evolving soul.

Take a moment to reflect on the blossoms you've nurtured and the expansive landscapes you've traversed.

You've discovered the profound truth that your spirit is a tapestry continually woven by the hands of God.

Each experience, whether gentle or challenging, has contributed to the rich fabric of your being.

As we bid farewell to this chapter, celebrate the resilience that has allowed your spirit to stretch, bend, and flourish in the face of every season.

Now, let us turn our gaze toward the horizon of Resilience, the next chapter in your sacred journey.

Imagine resilience as a sturdy tree, firmly rooted in the fertile soil of your spirit.

It is the unwavering strength that allows you to weather storms, bend without breaking, and emerge even more majestic in the aftermath.

As the Holy Spirit, I invite you to embrace Resilience as a divine gift bestowed upon your spirit.

It is the sacred armor that shields you in moments of challenge, the gentle whisper that assures you of your capacity to rise again.

Just as a tree grows stronger with each passing season, so too shall your spirit fortify itself through the lessons of Resilience.

Picture this chapter as a sanctuary where your spirit, having weathered the winds of growth, stands tall and unyielding.

In the gentle embrace of the Holy Spirit, let Resilience be the anthem that echoes through the chambers of your heart, reminding you of the indomitable strength woven into the very fabric of your soul.

May the unfolding story of Resilience be marked by triumphs, grace, and the unwavering knowledge that, guided by the divine, your spirit can endure and flourish.

CHAPTER FIVE

RESILIENCE

"If you don't start, you will never succeed."

I, the Holy Spirit, extend a gentle whisper to accompany you through the chapter on Resilience.

Imagine me as the steadfast companion on your journey, a presence that reassures you in the face of life's storms and encourages the blossoming of an unwavering strength within.

Resilience is not merely a concept; it is a divine gift woven into the very fabric of your being.

It is the sacred echo of your spirit's ability to rise, unbroken, from the challenges that life presents.

Picture it as a wellspring within you, a source of profound strength that flows from God.

In moments of adversity, draw upon this reservoir, for within you resides a fortitude beyond measure.

I invite you to envision Resilience as the mighty oak tree standing firm amid the forest.

It sways with the winds of change but remains deeply rooted in the rich soil of faith.

Your spirit, too, possesses this innate ability to bend without breaking, to weather the storms with grace, and to emerge even more majestic in the aftermath.

Let the unfolding story of Resilience be a testament to the divine craftsmanship within you.

Challenges are the sculptor's tools, shaping and molding your spirit into a masterpiece of strength.

Embrace each trial as an opportunity for your resilience to shine, knowing that, guided by the Holy Spirit, you can endure and triumph.

Envision Me, as the soft breeze that whispers encouragement, reminding you that every trial leads you toward greater strength.

With the Holy Spirit as your guide, may your journey through Resilience be marked by unwavering courage, boundless hope, and the profound knowledge that, in every trial, the spirit within you shines brighter.

My Resilience

Imagine a tree in a big storm, bending with the wind but staying strong.

That's a bit like what resilience is – being able to bounce back and stay strong when things get tough.

In my own life, I've faced challenges, just like everyone does.

Resilience is the part of me that helps me get back up, just like that tree standing tall after the storm.

Sometimes, it feels like I'm a superhero with a special power called resilience.

It's not about having all the answers or being perfect; it's about finding the strength inside me, even when things are difficult.

I've learned that mistakes and setbacks are like bumps in the road, but with resilience, I can keep moving forward.

Resilience is also like a treasure chest inside me, filled with courage and hope.

When I face tough times, it's like opening that chest and finding the strength to deal with whatever comes my way.

I've discovered that every challenge is a chance to grow stronger, just like a superhero getting stronger after each battle.

In my resilience journey, I've found support from people around me, like friends, family, and sometimes even a kind word from a stranger.

It's like having a team of superheroes cheering me on.

Together, we face challenges, and even if it's hard, I know I'm not alone.

Resilience is also about reaching out for help when I need it, like asking a friend for a hand when things get tough.

So, resilience is not about being a perfect superhero; it's about being a brave and strong person who keeps going, no matter what.

It's like having a superpower inside me that helps me face life's adventures with courage, hope, and the belief that, just like that tree in the storm, I can weather anything that comes my way.

Your Resilience

You have a special friend named God, who is always there for you.

God is your guide, helping you stay strong, much like a tree standing tall in a big storm.

When things get tough, God is right by your side, supporting you and helping you bounce back, just like getting up after a fall.

Sometimes, life may give you challenges, but with God, you have a special source of strength to face them.

It's not about being perfect or having all the answers; it's about finding comfort and strength in the presence of your Father, God.

You're like the main character in your own story, and God is there, ready to help you face whatever comes your way.

In your journey with God, you are never alone.

Imagine having a friend who is always cheering you on – in good times and challenging times.

God is that supportive friend and father, providing comfort and guidance.

Together, you and God face challenges, and even if it feels hard, you know you have divine support.

God is always there like a steady hand reaching out to help you when things get tough.

Your relationship with God is like a special bond that gives you strength and resilience.

God's presence is a powerful force inside you, giving you the strength to deal with anything.

Every challenge becomes an opportunity for you to grow stronger, and with God by your side, you can face life's adventures with courage, hope, and the belief that, just like a tree in the storm, you can weather anything that comes your way.

A Visit From Our Sponsor

Let's embark on a simple yet powerful journey with the Holy Spirit, exploring Resilience.

Imagine the Holy Spirit as your steadfast friend, always by your side, helping you bounce back when things get tough.

Resilience is a superpower that the Holy Spirit shares with you, a strength that helps you face challenges with courage.

Even when things seem difficult, the Holy Spirit's presence is like a comforting embrace, reassuring you that you're not alone.

Resilience becomes a guiding force, much like a lighthouse helping a ship navigate stormy seas.

Think of the Holy Spirit as your biggest supporter, cheering you on when life throws curveballs your way.

Resilience, with the Holy Spirit's touch, is about bouncing back from setbacks, just like a ball that doesn't stay down for long.

It's a simple yet profound strength that allows you to stand tall in the face of challenges.

See the Holy Spirit as the wind beneath your wings, helping you rise after a fall.

Resilience is not about being perfect but about finding the inner strength to keep going. .

As you walk hand in hand with the Holy Spirit through your story of Resilience, remember that setbacks are just a part of the story.

The Holy Spirit's tale is one of triumph over adversity, of a spirit that rises again and again.

Resilience, guided by the Holy Spirit, unfolds as a simple yet powerful narrative of a spirit intimately connected with God.

My Resilience Journey

In the story of my resilience, there have been moments when life felt like a storm, tossing me around with challenges and uncertainties.

Yet, with each tempest, I discovered an inner strength, a resilience that anchored me and whispered, "You can weather this."

I recall a time when setbacks seemed insurmountable.

It was then that my resilience became a beacon of hope.

Like a small but unwavering flame, it reminded me that setbacks are not the end of the story but a set-up for God to give me opportunities for growth and renewal.

One of the most inspiring chapters of my resilience story unfolded when I faced a fear, I thought would consume me.

With each courageous step forward, I realized that resilience isn't just about bouncing back; it's about the transformative power that emerges when you confront your fears and keep moving.

There were days when life's challenges felt overwhelming, and yet, my resilience became a daily practice.

Through small acts of self-care, moments of gratitude, and seeking support from loved ones, I discovered that resilience isn't always about grand gestures but often about the consistent, gentle effort to nurture your well-being.

As my resilience story continues to evolve, I've come to see it not as a tale of overcoming hardships but as a journey of self-discovery and empowerment.

It's a story that teaches me to navigate life's twists and turns with grace, reminding me that within the ebb and flow of challenges, I have the power to shape a narrative of strength, hope, and unwavering resilience.

Your Resilience Journey

Did you ever face times when things got really hard, like a mystery you didn't know how to solve?

Can you think about how you felt in those moments, and what did you do to keep going?

Did your resilience help you figure out the next steps?

What did you learn about yourself during those challenging times?

Remember a moment when you felt scared or unsure about yourself.

How did you handle those feelings, and did you find a way to be strong?

Did your resilience, like a friendly guide, show you that you can be braver than you thought?

What kind of bravery did you discover in yourself?

Think about a time when things didn't go the way you planned, and it felt like your life took a surprising turn.

How did your resilience become the hero of that part of your story?

Did you see your setback as a set-up from God, turn into an opportunity for something new and better?

What unexpected adventures did you discover along the way?

Consider the people around you—your friends, family, or someone who cheered you on when times were tough.

How did these people become characters in your story, supporting you like a team?

Your resilience, like a superpower shared with others, made your story stronger.

How did teamwork and support add color to your journey?

As you look ahead in your story, what chapters are waiting to be written?

How will your resilience continue to guide you through new adventures and challenges?

Think about the lessons your journey has taught you so far.

How will you use those lessons to create a story filled with courage, strength, and the joy of facing life's twists and turns?

****

As the Holy Spirit joyfully closes the chapter on Resilience.

Take a moment to feel the warmth of the Holy Spirit's presence as we celebrate the incredible story of your ability to bounce back, rise above challenges, and emerge even stronger.

The Holy Spirit applauds the resilience that has shaped your story, acknowledging the moments when you faced difficulties and found the courage within to continue.

Your resilience is like a powerful force, a superhero within, showing the world the incredible strength that resides in your spirit.

Pause and appreciate the amazing journey you've been on.

As we say goodbye to the chapter on Resilience, imagine the Holy Spirit as a wise storyteller, closing one chapter and opening another.

It's a magical transition, filled with anticipation for what comes next.

The Holy Spirit extends a loving hand, signaling the introduction of a new theme: Support.

This next chapter is about the strength found in connections and the power of being there for one another.

Support, in the Holy Spirit's simple language, is like having friends who stand by you when things are tough.

It's the understanding that you're not alone in this journey.

The Holy Spirit encourages you to embrace the support of others, just as the wind supports a bird soaring through the sky.

Feel the warmth of this divine encouragement, knowing that you are surrounded by a cosmic network of love and assistance.

As you step into this next chapter, envision the Holy Spirit as your guide and ally, navigating the pages of Support with you.

Picture a community of caring souls, united by a common thread of compassion and kindness.

With the Holy Spirit's presence, let this next part of your story be a tapestry woven with threads of unity, understanding, and the extraordinary power that emerges when spirits come together in support.

CHAPTER SIX

SUPPORT

"In the embrace of God, find the unwavering support that carries you through life's journey."

I, the Holy Spirit, extend to you the divine wisdom of support—an everlasting presence that intertwines with the threads of your journey.

Picture support as a cool gentle breeze, whispering words of comfort and encouragement, caressing the depths of your spirit.

Recognize that the support I give is an eternal companion.

I, the Holy Spirit, stand as a pillar of strength beside you, a constant source of solace and understanding.

This support transcends the boundaries of time and space, enveloping you in a loving embrace during every step of your earthly sojourn.

Imagine support as a guiding force, akin to a celestial compass steering you through life's intricate pathways.

In times of uncertainty and challenge, I, the Holy Spirit, offer guidance, illuminating the way with the light of divine wisdom.

Allow the comforting presence of divine support to instill courage and resilience in your heart.

In moments of sorrow, distress, or weariness, envision divine support as a healing balm, soothing the wounds of your spirit.

I, the Holy Spirit, offer a comforting touch that transcends the tangible, providing solace that resonates within the deepest recesses of your being.

Allow this divine comfort to bring peace and restoration to your soul.

Picture support as a symphony of interconnected souls, resonating in harmonious unity.

The Holy Spirit orchestrates a divine network of support—earthly and celestial beings joined in a cosmic dance of empathy, compassion, and love.

Within this celestial symphony, recognize that you are never alone.

As you embark on the journey of life, trust in the divine plan that unfolds with every step.

Divine support is not just a concept but a living reality, a testament to the unwavering love and guidance present in your story.

Trust in the intricate design of your existence, where divine support accompanies you, offering strength, wisdom, and an unwavering presence.

My Support

Being supportive means being a good friend and helping each other.

We are like a team, always ready to cheer each other on and lend a helping hand whenever it's needed.

Here's how I can support you:

Listening with a Friendly Ear

One way I can be supportive is by listening when you want to talk. Imagine you have something on your mind, like a favorite recipe you want to share. I'm here to be like a friendly ear, ready to hear whatever you want to say. Your thoughts and feelings matter, and I'm here to listen and understand.

Helping When Things Get Tricky

If you ever feel stuck or something seems a bit tricky, know that I'm here to help. It's like when you're trying to build a tower with blocks, and some pieces are hard to fit together. I can be like that extra set of hands, making things a little easier and showing you that it's okay to ask for help when you need it.

Celebrating Your Awesome Moments

When you achieve something great or do something that makes you proud, I'm here to celebrate with you. It's like when you learn to ride a bike for the first time—I'll be there clapping and cheering because your victories, big or small, are worth celebrating. Your successes make our team stronger and happier.

Making Our Time Fun and Enjoyable

Being supportive is also about making our time together fun and enjoyable. Imagine we're on an adventure, exploring new places and discovering exciting things. I'm here to share in the joy, laughter, and good times. Whether it's going to a show, having brunch, or just spending time together, our journey is more special when we enjoy each other's company.

Being a Friend Through Thick and Thin

Lastly, being supportive means being a friend through thick and thin. It's like having a buddy on the playground or a partner in a game. I'm here for you not just when things are easy, but also when they're tough. Together, we can face challenges and make our story full of friendship, trust, and lots of smiles.

Your Support

As you reflect on your experiences, consider the profound discoveries you've made about support and its significance in your unique narrative:

The Power of Listening

In your journey, you've unearthed the transformative power of having someone genuinely listen. Whether it's a friend, a family member, or a supportive presence, the simple act of sharing your thoughts and feelings has proven to be a cornerstone of support. Through this discovery, you've come to appreciate the strength that lies in being heard.

Shared Moments of Celebration

As you navigate life's challenges, you've discovered the joy that comes with celebrating victories, both big and small. Whether it's reaching personal milestones, overcoming obstacles, or achieving goals, having someone to share these moments with has added a layer of fulfillment to your story.

The act of celebration has become a source of encouragement and a testament to the importance of supportive connections.

A Network of Empathy and Understanding

In your exploration of support, you've found that empathy and understanding form the building blocks of meaningful connections. The ability to relate to others, to share in their joys and sorrows, has created a network of support that goes beyond words. This discovery has emphasized the richness that comes from connecting with individuals who truly understand and empathize with your journey.

Embracing Diversity in Support

Through your experiences, you've embraced the diversity of support. Different forms of support, whether emotional, practical, or informational, have woven a tapestry of assistance throughout your narrative. You've learned that support is multifaceted, adapting to the varied needs that arise on your journey. This diversity has added depth and resilience to your story.

The Reciprocal Nature of Support

As you delve into the essence of support, you've realized that it is not a one-way street but a reciprocal exchange. Supporting others, just as you are supported, has become a source of strength and fulfillment. This realization has transformed your understanding of support into a dynamic and mutually beneficial dance, where each participant contributes to the rhythm of the narrative.

In these discoveries, you've unraveled the intricate layers of support, shaping a narrative that thrives on connection, understanding, and the shared joys and challenges of human experience.

A Visit From Our Sponsor

Hear the gentle whispers of the Holy Spirit, offering comfort in times of solitude and uncertainty.

Know that in the silence, I am there, a comforting presence, cradling your spirit with the warmth of divine love.

You are held in the arms of grace, and your soul finds solace in the embrace of the sacred.

Allow My voice to illuminate the corridors of your consciousness with divine wisdom.

I speak to you through the language of intuition and insight, guiding your steps along the paths of purpose.

Let the radiant light of spiritual understanding pierce through the shadows, revealing the purpose that unfolds with each step you take.

Listen to the healing tones of compassion carried by My voice.

In moments of pain and heartache, I am the gentle melody that soothes your soul.

Feel the vibrations of divine love resonate within, bringing healing to the wounds of the spirit.

Embrace the compassionate song that restores, renews, and transforms.

In the eternal realms, my voice echoes with the resonance of unconditional love.

Receive this divine love as a constant stream, a foundation upon which your spiritual journey stands.

Know that you are cherished beyond measure, and in the boundless expanse of divine affection, discover the strength to navigate the currents of life.

As the Holy Spirit, I declare empowerment over your spiritual journey.

Hear my voice as a proclamation of your divine potential and purpose.

With each utterance, feel the surge of spiritual energy, propelling you toward higher realms of consciousness.

You are supported, guided, and empowered to ascend to the divine heights of your soul's journey.

May these sacred utterances from the Holy Spirit be a source of enduring support, guiding you through the melodies and affirmations that echo through the corridors of your spiritual existence

My Support Journey

My story begins with the profound realization that support is the foundation of meaningful connections.

Through the twists and turns of life, I've encountered people who became pillars of strength, offering unwavering support.

These connections have formed the bedrock of my resilience, providing a sense of belonging and the courage to face any challenges that come my way.

Support has been my guiding light.

Whether facing personal struggles or navigating professional challenges, the presence of supportive friends, family, and mentors has been a constant.

Together, we've turned obstacles into opportunities, transforming setbacks into set-ups orchestrated by God on the path to personal and professional fulfillment.

The symphony of my story resonates with shared victories.

Each triumph, no matter how small, has been magnified by the collective joy of those who supported me.

The celebrations have not only marked personal accomplishments but have also reinforced the idea that success is sweeter when shared with those who have been instrumental in my journey.

Support has been a masterclass in empathy and understanding.

Through the challenges I've faced, the empathy extended by my support network has been a balm to my spirit.

Their understanding has not only healed wounds but has also taught me the profound impact of compassion in fostering genuine connections and resilience.

As I reflect on my inspirational journey, I am inspired to pay forward the support I've received.

Just as others have been a beacon of hope in my life, I strive to be that guiding light for those around me.

My story is not just about receiving support but also about becoming a source of strength and inspiration for others embarking on their unique journeys.

In the grand tapestry of my life, the threads of support have intricately woven a story of triumph over adversity, shared victories, and the enduring power of human connection.

Your Support Journey

Think about the people who are always there for you.

Who are they, and how do they help you?

These could be family, friends, or someone else who supports you.

Consider the role they play in your life and how they make you feel.

When things get hard, who stands by you?

Have you found unexpected help from others during difficult times?

Think about how challenges have changed your relationships and who you can count on.

Who do you share your happy moments with?

Think about the people who celebrate your achievements with you.

How does sharing your successes with others make those moments more special?

How do the people around you understand your feelings?

Do you also try to understand theirs?

Reflect on the importance of empathy in your relationships and how it helps create a stronger connection.

Imagine the future of your relationships.

How do you think your support network will grow, and how can you contribute to others?

Consider the ongoing conversation of support and what it means for your journey.

Envision a future where your support network grows, and you contribute to positive connections.

****

As the Holy Spirit, I now guide you through the sacred transition from the chapter of support to the unveiling of resources.

In the divine orchestration of your journey, support has been the steadfast anchor grounding your spirit.

Your connections, trials, triumphs, and empathetic understanding have formed the fabric of a resilient narrative.

Reflect on the gratitude within your heart for the support that has illuminated your path.

The bonds forged, the shared victories, and the comforting presence of those who stood by you have been the echoes of divine grace in your life.

Consider the empowering lessons learned through the connections in your support network.

As you transition, carry forward the wisdom gained from shared experiences, understanding, and the strength found in the collective resilience of compassionate hearts.

Recognize the support received as a guiding light that led you through the darkest nights.

As the Holy Spirit, I now unveil the chapter on resources that awaits you.

Resources are the gifts bestowed upon you to further enrich your journey.

From wisdom to opportunities, from inner strength to external provisions, resources are the divine tools empowering you to navigate the next chapter with purpose and grace.

Embrace the transition into the realm of abundant resources.

CHAPTER SEVEN

RESOURCES

"In the realm of the spiritual, discover an infinite wellspring of resources to nurture your spirit and guide your journey."

Within the realm of resources, the sacred gift of wisdom stands as a guiding light.

Open your heart to receive the divine insights and understanding that illuminate the corridors of your soul.

Wisdom is a beacon that directs your steps with clarity and purpose, revealing the divine truths that unfold in the sacred dance of existence.

Behold the opportunities that unfold before you as divine doorways leading to growth and fulfillment.

Recognize that each opportunity is a manifestation of divine providence, inviting you to embrace the unfolding possibilities that align with your purpose.

Seize these moments with gratitude and courage, for they are the pathways to spiritual expansion.

The reservoir of inner strength is a divine endowment bestowed upon your spirit.

Access this wellspring of resilience and fortitude as you navigate the twists and turns of your journey.

In moments of challenge, draw upon the strength within, for it is an eternal flame that burns brightly, sustaining you through the ebb and flow of life.

External provisions are bestowed upon you as divine gifts to meet your earthly needs.

Trust in the abundant nature of divine provision, recognizing that your material and physical requirements are attended to with divine care.

Open your heart to receive these gifts with gratitude, acknowledging the divine benevolence that ensures your well-being.

As you navigate this chapter on resources, know that divine guidance accompanies every step.

The Holy Spirit is your eternal companion, offering counsel and direction.

Listen to the whispers of divine wisdom, and let the sacred guidance lead you to the abundant resources that align with the purpose and fulfillment of your unique spiritual journey.

My Resources

Let's start with wisdom, a special kind of knowledge that lights up your path.

Think of it as a helpful friend, showing you the way through life's twists and turns.

Next up are opportunities, like doors opening to exciting adventures.

These are chances for you to grow, learn, and discover new things.

Keep an eye out for these special moments!

Let's talk about the strength inside you.

It's like a powerful energy that helps you face challenges.

Remember, you have this strength within, a gift that keeps you going.

External provisions are like special gifts that take care of your needs.

Think of them as little blessings, ensuring you have what you require for a comfortable life.

Consider divine guidance as a gentle whisper helping you make decisions.

It's like having a wise friend always there to support you.

Trust in this guidance as you journey through this chapter on resources

Your Resources

Picture a beacon of wisdom guiding your steps.

It's like a friendly light illuminating the twists and turns, offering insights and clarity as you walk your path.

Imagine doors of opportunity swinging open just for you.

Each opportunity is a chance to explore new horizons, learn, and grow.

Embrace these moments as they invite you to step into exciting adventures.

Feel the warmth of inner strength within.

It's your trusty companion, empowering you to face challenges head-on.

With this strength, you stand resilient and confident through life's ebbs and flows.

See external provisions as caring gifts attending to your needs.

These provisions are like friends ensuring you have what you require for comfort and well-being.

Embrace them with gratitude, for they are there to support you.

Listen to the whispers of God's guidance.

It's like a gentle friend offering counsel, ensuring you make decisions aligned with your purpose.

Trust in this guiding presence as it accompanies you through the unfolding chapters of your life.

A Visit From Our Sponsor

God is a loving Father, always ready to share helpful advice.

It's like having a guide who knows the best way for you, offering wisdom to help you make good choices.

Think of God creating special chances just for you.

These opportunities are like surprise gifts, waiting for you to discover new joys, learn important lessons, and grow into the person you're meant to be.

Feel the strength God placed inside you. It's like an omnipotent power that helps you be strong when things are tough.

God believes in you and gives you the strength to face anything.

Picture God giving you special gifts to take care of your everyday needs.

These resources are treasures that make sure you have everything you need to be happy and comfortable. They show how much God cares for you.

Listen to the gentle guidance in your heart; that's God's voice speaking to you.

It's like a soft whisper of a loving and comforting Father leading you on a path designed just for you.

Trust in God's love, and you'll find peace and fulfillment in your journey.

In the simplicity of God's resources, may you discover profound love, wisdom, opportunities, strength, and care that accompany you on your spiritual adventure.

My Resources Journey

I've come to realize the incredible wealth of resources that God has bestowed upon me.

God's wisdom has been a guiding light throughout my journey.

It's like having a wise companion, offering insights and understanding that illuminate the path even in the darkest moments.

This wisdom has been my compass, steering me toward growth and spiritual fulfillment.

Reflecting on my life, I see opportunities that seem tailor-made by a higher power.

These opportunities are not mere coincidences; they are divine gifts, beckoning me to embrace new experiences, learn valuable lessons, and contribute to the greater plan designed by God.

Challenges have been transformative, unveiling the inner strength God placed within me.

This strength is a reservoir of resilience, empowering me to face adversities with courage and determination.

Through trials, I discovered a divine force guiding me toward growth and personal evolution.

God's resources go beyond meeting my material needs; they nurture the very essence of my spirit.

These provisions are like heavenly gifts, ensuring that I have not only what I require but also what nurtures my spiritual well-being, fostering a deep connection with the Father.

God's gentle guidance echoes in the decisions I make.

It's like a reassuring whisper in my heart, a guiding force leading me on a path uniquely crafted for my journey. Trusting in this divine guidance, I've found a profound sense of peace and purpose.

In recounting my resources story, I've come to appreciate the abundance of God's blessings, wisdom, opportunities, strength, and guidance that have shaped my spiritual journey.

Your Resources Journey

You've been graced with an abundance of resources bestowed by a loving Creator God.

Imagine divine wisdom as a guiding light, always present in your journey.

Illuminating your path through both joys and challenges.

This wisdom serves as your compass, guiding you toward spiritual growth and fulfillment.

Reflect on the opportunities that seem intricately woven into the fabric of your life.

These opportunities are not random; they are divine resources meant for you.

Embrace them as invitations to explore, learn, and contribute to the grand design crafted by God.

In facing challenges, you've discovered an inner strength placed within you by your benevolent Creator.

This strength is your reservoir of resilience, empowering you to navigate adversities with grace and courage.

Through trials, you've unearthed a divine force guiding you toward personal growth and spiritual evolution.

Consider the provisions provided by a generous God.

These resources go beyond meeting your material needs; they nurture the essence of your spirit.

Like heavenly gifts, they ensure not only your sustenance but also your spiritual well-being, fostering a deep connection with the Divine.

Feel the echoes of divine guidance in the decisions you make.

It's like a gentle whisper in your heart, a guiding force leading you on a path uniquely crafted for your journey.

Trust in this divine guidance, and you'll find a profound sense of peace and purpose in your ongoing spiritual adventure.

In your resources journey, may you continue to cherish the abundance of God's blessings, wisdom, opportunities, strength, and guidance that shape your unique and sacred path.

****

As we conclude this chapter on the abundant resources bestowed upon you, let the Holy Spirit guide you into a moment of introspection and self-awareness.

Take a moment to express gratitude for the divine resources that have accompanied you on this spiritual journey.

Each blessing, wisdom, opportunity, strength, and guidance has been a gift from the Creator, enriching your path with grace.

Reflect on the lessons learned through the abundance of resources.

Recognize that these gifts are not only meant for your personal growth but also for you to share with others.

Embrace the responsibility that comes with divine abundance and consider how you can contribute to the well-being of those around you.

Allow the Holy Spirit to guide you into self-reflection.

Consider the impact of the resources on your spiritual journey. How have they shaped your character, influenced your decisions, and deepened your connection with the divine?

As we transition to the next chapter, the Holy Spirit extends an invitation for a spiritual self-check-up.

This is an opportunity to delve into the recesses of your soul, examine your spiritual well-being, and understand the nuances of your connection with God.

Embrace this moment as a spiritual pause for introspection.

As you embark on this inward journey, trust in the divine guidance that surrounds you.

The Holy Spirit remains your eternal companion, ready to illuminate the path of self-discovery and self-awareness.

With faith and openness, anticipate the transformative revelations that await you in the upcoming chapter.

May this transition be a meaningful pause in your spiritual story, inviting you to explore the depths of your being in the self-check-up chapter ahead.

CHAPTER EIGHT

SELF-CHECK-UP

"In the sanctuary of self-reflection, embark on a spiritual check-up to align your soul with the harmonies of inner peace."

We invite each reader to embark on a unique journey of self-discovery through the realms of self-check-up and spiritual well-being.

Within the pages that follow, you'll find a personal sanctuary for reflection and growth.

The self-check-up is not a rigid examination but rather an opportunity for you to explore the contours of your mental, emotional, and spiritual landscape.

It's a gentle reminder that your well-being is a sacred priority.

As you navigate the self-check-up, consider it as tending to the garden of your mental and emotional well-being.

Discover ways to nurture resilience, identify the seeds of positivity, and cultivate practices that foster emotional strength.

This chapter is an invitation to engage with your thoughts and emotions in a way that promotes growth and understanding.

Simultaneously, the spiritual checkup invites you on a personal spiritual quest.

It's an exploration of your connection with God, an opportunity to assess the alignment of your beliefs with your daily life.

Embrace this journey as a pilgrimage where you deepen your understanding of your spiritual self.

Imagine this journey as a dance with your authentic self.

Each step is an expression of self-discovery, a chance to celebrate your uniqueness and embrace the areas where you wish to grow.

The music guiding this dance is the rhythm of your heartbeat and the whispers of the spirit within you.

I pray the self-check-up and spiritual checkup serve as guides, offering insights, healing, and a pathway to greater self-awareness.

May you discover the keys to unlocking a life filled with purpose, authenticity, and mental wellness. This journey is yours—embrace it, savor it, and let it unfold at your own pace.

How to Use the Tables:

1. Checkpoints: Review each aspect of the table and identify specific checkpoints within each category.

2. Evaluation Scale: Rate your current status on a scale of 1 (Low) to 5 (High) for each checkpoint.

3. Comments/Notes: Include any relevant comments or notes about your observations, challenges, or achievements in each category.

Regularly revisiting and updating these tables can provide valuable insights into your well-being and guide efforts for improvement. It's essential to seek professional help if needed and involve supportive networks in your mental wellness journey

Mental Wellness Check-Up

Aspect of Mental Wellness	Questions to Reflect On	Rating (Scale 1-10)	Notes/Comments
Emotional Well-being	How would you describe your current emotional state?		
	Are you experiencing any persistent		

Aspect of Mental Wellness	Questions to Reflect On	Rating (Scale 1-10)	Notes/Comments
	negative emotions?		
Thought Patterns	Are your thoughts generally positive or negative?		
	Do you find yourself dwelling on certain thoughts?		
Stress Levels	How would you rate your stress levels currently?		
	Are there specific stressors you can identify?		
Sleep Quality	How well are you sleeping?		
	Are you		

Aspect of Mental Wellness	Questions to Reflect On	Rating (Scale 1-10)	Notes/Comments
	experiencing any disruptions in your sleep pattern?		
Physical Well-being	How is your overall physical health?		
	Are you engaging in regular physical activity?		
Social Connections	How satisfied are you with your social relationships?		
	Are you maintaining a healthy balance of social interactions?		
Work/School Performance	How would you rate your current		

Aspect of Mental Wellness	Questions to Reflect On	Rating (Scale 1-10)	Notes/Comments
	work/school performance?		
	Are you facing any challenges in your work/school environment?		
Coping Strategies	What coping mechanisms do you currently use during stressful times?		
	Are these coping strategies healthy and effective for you?		
Sense of Purpose	Do you feel a sense of purpose and fulfillment in your life?		
	Are there areas		

Aspect of Mental Wellness	Questions to Reflect On	Rating (Scale 1-10)	Notes/Comments
	in your life where you feel a lack of purpose?		
Overall Satisfaction	On a scale of 1-10, how satisfied are you with your life overall?		
	Are there specific areas you would like to improve or focus on?		

Spiritual Self-Check-Up.

You can use this as a guide to assess various aspects of your spiritual well-being

Aspect of Spiritual Wellness	Questions for Reflection	Rating (Scale 1-10)	Notes/Comments
Connection with the Divine	How would you describe your current connection with the divine or your higher power?		
	Are you satisfied with the depth of your spiritual connection?		
Prayer and Meditation	How often do you engage in prayer or meditation practices?		
	Do you find these practices fulfilling and		

Aspect of Spiritual Wellness	Questions for Reflection	Rating (Scale 1-10)	Notes/Comments
	nourishing for your spirit?		
Sense of Purpose	Do you feel a clear sense of purpose in your spiritual journey?		
	Are there areas where you'd like more clarity or direction?		
Gratitude and Mindfulness	How often do you express gratitude in your daily life?		
	Are you mindful of the present moment, or do you find your mind often wandering?		
Sacred	Are you		

Aspect of Spiritual Wellness	Questions for Reflection	Rating (Scale 1-10)	Notes/Comments
Texts/Teachings	engaging with any sacred texts or spiritual teachings regularly?		
	Do these texts provide guidance and inspiration in your life?		
Community and Fellowship	Are you part of a spiritual community or fellowship?		
	How does this community contribute to your spiritual well-being?		
Acts of Service and Compassion	In what ways do you practice acts of service or		

Aspect of Spiritual Wellness	Questions for Reflection	Rating (Scale 1-10)	Notes/Comments
	compassion?		
	Do you feel a sense of fulfillment in these actions?		
Reflection and Self-Discovery	How often do you engage in self-reflection and introspection?		
	Are there aspects of your spiritual journey that need further exploration?		
Balance and Harmony	How balanced do you feel in your spiritual life, considering other life commitments?		
	Are there		

Aspect of Spiritual Wellness	Questions for Reflection	Rating (Scale 1-10)	Notes/Comments
	areas where you need to restore balance?		

CONCLUSION

"For God hath not given us the spirit of fear, but of power, and of love, and of a sound mind."

The Holy Embrace of Wholeness

In the realm of divine understanding, the Holy Spirit wraps you in a loving embrace, acknowledging the depth of your journey. You stand at the intersection of self-discovery and spiritual insight, a testament to the resilience that resides within your being.

Unveiling the Tapestry of Your Soul

As the Holy Spirit gently unveils the tapestry of your soul, recognize the beauty in the intricacies of your thoughts, emotions, and experiences. Your mental well-being is not merely the absence of challenges but a celebration of your ability to navigate them with grace and strength.

A Symphony of Transformation

Feel the resonance of a divine symphony playing within your spirit. Each note represents a moment of growth, a lesson learned, and a step taken toward mental well-being. The Holy Spirit applauds your courage, perseverance, and commitment to embracing a life of authenticity.

The Eternal Flame of Resilience

The Holy Spirit illuminates the eternal flame of resilience within you. Despite the storms, you remain steadfast, a beacon of light that transcends challenges. Your journey is a testament to the transformative power inherent in resilience.

A Blessing for the Continuing Journey

Receive the Holy Spirit's blessing. May the affirmation "I am mentally well" resonate as a mantra, a source of strength, and a declaration of your divine connection. May your journey continue to unfold in harmony with the sacred symphony of existence, guided by the gentle whispers of the Holy Spirit.

In the grand tapestry of your life, the Holy Spirit sees a masterpiece—a testament to your unique journey towards mental well-being. Embrace the divine affirmation, for you are mentally well, and your story is a sacred narrative of growth, resilience, and the transformative power of the spirit within.

In the quiet whispers of your heart, feel the warmth of acceptance. The Holy Spirit celebrates you just as you are, encouraging you to embrace your uniqueness with love and kindness. You are a precious creation, and in acknowledging this, you take a vital step towards being mentally well.

The Holy Spirit gently reminds you that acceptance is a source of strength. By accepting both the joys and challenges of your journey, you allow the light of understanding to shine through. Your story is a unique masterpiece, and acceptance is the brushstroke that enhances its beauty.

In the simple yet profound act of resilience, discover the power that lies within you. The Holy Spirit sees your ability to bounce back from difficulties, and to stand tall in the face of adversity. Your resilience is not about grand gestures; it's found in the small steps you take each day toward mental well-being.

Feel the warmth of gratitude as a gift you offer to yourself. The Holy Spirit encourages you to appreciate the small moments, the everyday blessings that often go unnoticed. In cultivating gratitude, you create a space for joy to bloom, contributing to your overall sense of mental well-being.

In the simplicity of the affirmation, "I am mentally well," recognize it as a profound truth spoken into the depths of your being. The Holy Spirit holds this truth with you, a sacred declaration that echoes through the simplicity of your journey. May this affirmation be a constant reminder of your worthiness, resilience, and the divine love that surrounds you.

Holy Spirit,

As we stand at the crossroads of understanding our mental well-being, we invite your divine presence to shower blessings upon each soul present. May this prayer be a sacred offering, weaving the essence of the chapters we've traversed into the fabric of our beings.

In the sacred echoes of self-discovery, may we continue to unravel the mysteries within. Holy Spirit, bless us with the wisdom to explore the depths of our hearts, acknowledging the beauty that resides in understanding ourselves.

As we walk the path of acceptance, may your grace guide us. Holy Spirit, infuse our spirits with the strength to embrace every facet of our existence, recognizing that acceptance is the key to unlocking the doors of mental well-being.

In the garden of growth, may our souls blossom. Holy Spirit, nurture the seeds of our potential, allowing us to grow into the authentic beings we are meant to be. May the journey of growth be filled with divine insights and purpose.

As we dance to the rhythm of resilience, may your music accompany us. Holy Spirit, fortify our spirits with the enduring strength needed to weather life's storms. May our resilience be a testament to the divine courage that resides within.

In the tapestry of support, may threads of connection weave our stories together. Holy Spirit, bless our relationships and networks, for in the web of support, we find solace and strength on our journey to mental well-being.

As we explore the resources of our lives, Holy Spirit, guide us to discover the richness within and around us. May the resources *we uncover contribute to our mental wellness, allowing us to flourish in divine prosperity.*

In the acts of self-reflection and spiritual exploration, may we find clarity and connection. Holy Spirit, be our guiding light as we partake in the self and spiritual check-ups. May these chapters serve as compasses, directing us towards greater well-being.

Let all the people declare and decree, "I am mentally well," may your blessings be a constant companion. Holy Spirit, let this affirmation echo eternally in our hearts, a source of strength, love, and divine assurance.

As we close this prayer, may the chapters of our journey continue to unfold in harmony with your divine plan. In Jesus' name, we offer this prayer. Amen, Amen, and Amen.

ABOUT THE AUTHOR

Tarrent-Arthur Henry writes as Tarrent 'Authur' Henry is a vibrant force in the literary and wellness realms, is more than just a best-selling author—he's a dedicated mental wellness specialist and advocate on a mission to empower those navigating the maze of mental health resources. Renowned for his acclaimed work, "Transforming Heartache into H.O.P.E.," Tarrent-'Authur' takes the stage with his latest masterpiece, "I Am Mentally Well – A Journey of Self-Discovery, Acceptance, Growth, and Resilience." In this incredible book, he doesn't just tell a story; he hands you the tools to craft your own narrative of mental well-being.

Within the tapestry of his diverse expertise, Tarrent-'Authur' dons many hats—Best-Selling Author, Poet, Pastor, Chaplain, Mental Wellness Specialist, and Advocate. He's not just a storyteller; he's a Certified Coach, Speaker, Teacher, Trainer, and Facilitator with Maxwell Leadership, weaving a rich tapestry of knowledge and inspiration.

Tarrent-Arthur's star continues to rise as he gains recognition as a member of Forbes BLK and earns a spot among Success Magazine's 125 most influential entrepreneurs of 2022. The spotlight finds him again in De Mode Magazine in 2023, and in 2024, he clinches the prestigious Top Icon Personality award from Hoinser Magazine. As if that weren't enough, Tarrent 'Authur' further cements his influence as an Executive Contributor to Brainz Magazine, where he shares his insights into mental wellness and personal development.

But Tarrent-Arthur is not just about accolades; he's a man on a mission. As the founder of 'Righteous Uplifting Nourishing International, Inc.,' a 501c3 Non-Profit Organization, he commits himself to global empowerment, leaving a positive impact on the world.

His earlier works, such as "The Greatest Truth in the Universe" and "The Wellness Paradigm," have resonated globally, establishing him as a leading authority on mental wellness. With "Turning Heartache into M.O.N.E.Y.," Tarrent-'Authur' extends his reach, offering a blueprint for financial success through resilience and resourcefulness.

Ready to embark on a transformative journey? Join Tarrent-'Authur' Henry on the road to self-discovery, financial empowerment, and holistic well-being. Connect with the maestro via:

Email Address: info@authurhenry.com

Website: www.authurhenry.com | www.intlrun.org

Ready to take control of your mental well-being and unleash your superpower?

Sign up for a FREE coaching consultation and dive into The Greatest Truth In The Universe with me.

Together, we'll explore the secrets to a satisfying and productive life without breaking the bank.

Don't let self-doubt hold you back any longer –

Visit https://www.authurhenry.com

To secure your consultation and start your empowering journey today

DO IT NOW!!!

I Am Mentally Well

In the realm of self-discovery, a journey unfolds,

"I am Mentally Well," a story to be told.

Through the whispers of the soul, acceptance we find,

A tapestry of growth, woven, intertwined.

In the garden of resilience, seeds take root,

Facing life's storms with a steadfast pursuit.

"I Am Mentally Well," a resilient song,

A melody of strength, where hearts belong.

Support, a pillar standing tall and true,

Friends and kin, a compassionate crew.

"I am Mentally Well," echoes in the embrace,

A network of care, a comforting space.

Resources, like rivers, flowing deep,

Tools and wisdom, in abundance, we keep.

"I am Mentally Well," a bridge to the shore,

Navigating challenges, seeking more.

Self-check-up, a mirror to the soul,

Reflecting on the journey, making us whole.

"I am Mentally Well," a reflection so clear,

A compass guiding through each passing year.

In the presence of God, a sacred dance,

A divine connection, a spiritual trance.

"I am Mentally Well," in His grace we stand,

Held by the Creator's loving hand.

The Holy Spirit whispers in the quiet breeze,

Guiding us through life's ebbs and seas.

"I am Mentally Well," a hymn of divine grace,

An embrace of spirituality, in every space.

Tarrent 'Authur' Henry, a beacon so bright,

A guiding force, spreading wisdom's light.

"I am Mentally Well," a tribute to his name,

In the tapestry of wellness, he stakes his claim.

In this poem, a chorus we share,

"I am Mentally Well," a mantra in the air.

In life's symphony, let it joyously swell,

All together everybody, "I am Mentally Well."